CASTING
OUT

ESSENTIAL POETS SERIES 300

Guernica Editions Inc. acknowledges the support of
the Canada Council for the Arts and the Ontario Arts Council.
The Ontario Arts Council is an agency of the Government of Ontario.
We acknowledge the financial support of the Government of Canada

Rocco de Giacomo

CASTING OUT

GUERNICA
EDITIONS

TORONTO • CHICAGO • BUFFALO • LANCASTER (U.K.)
2023

Anna van Valkenburg, editor
Michael Mirolla, general editor
Cover and interior design: Rafael Chimicatti
Cover image: Marek Piwnicki, "Herbarium – Herb Robert"

Guernica Editions Inc.
287 Templemead Drive, Hamilton, (ON), Canada L8W 2W4
2250 Military Road, Tonawanda, N.Y. 14150-6000 U.S.A.
www.guernicaeditions.com

Distributors:
University of Toronto Press Distribution (UTP)
5201 Dufferin Street, Toronto (ON), Canada M3H 5T8
Independent Publishers Group (IPG)
814 N Franklin Street, Chicago, IL 60610, U.S.A.
Gazelle Book Services, White Cross Mills
High Town, Lancaster LA1 4XS U.K.

First edition.
Printed in Canada.

Legal Deposit – First Quarter
Library of Congress Catalog Card Number: 2022947042
Library and Archives Canada Cataloguing in Publication
Title: Casting out / Rocco de Giacomo.
Names: De Giacomo, Rocco, author.
Series: Essential poets ; 300.
Description: Series statement: Essential poets series ; 300
Identifiers: Canadiana 20220435480 | ISBN 9781771837699 (softcover)
Classification: LCC PS8557.E3684 C37 2023 | DDC C811/.6—dc23

For Lisa, who has never said no

to the question, "Can I read this to you?"

Contents

For Then Shall Be Great Tribulation

Bank cards are the beginning,
Mom says. *The Antichrist will make sure you can't buy food*
without his number tattooed on your arm.
Grandma sits beside me in the back seat;
says, *six, six, six*, as if completing
one of her crosswords. Dad pumps the gallons,
dwelling not on the opening
of the Seals of Judgement
nor on the sun turning black
as sackcloth, but the development
of prime real estate outside Wakefield,
Rhode Island. *They are already turning*
against Israel, Mom says. *Whatever*
you do, you must never, never, side against Zion.
Won't matter anyway, Grandma says, *we're all going*
to be taken up. Except your father, giggles Mom,
as he climbs up into the van; he doesn't respond
although he can guess, and this
has been a nine-hour drive
already. Goddammit, the end times
at a Sunoco in Cheektowaga. Is she gonna talk
about this all day? *For Christ's sake. Harriet, would ya stop,*
he'll eventually say
loudly, and maybe she'll stop.

Or she'll take a long sip
of her Pepsi through the straw, peer
down the remainder

of the I-95 and decide the rapture
could happen over the Peace Bridge.
And then, poor Vito—suddenly alone
in all that quiet.

Pat Robertson Tells Us

to touch the screen, says distance is no boundary
for the Holy Ghost. Mom leans close
to the cathode ray tube, touches it;
I hold hands with her and my big sister
as Pat leans into us. In a voice
like Virginian surf, he says, *May the anointing*
of the Holy Spirit
come upon you. He tells us
there is someone out there
with a bowel obstruction, in terrible pain. A knot
appears in Pat's brow. *You've been to the doctor's*
and nothing has worked. We pray for you now
and your intestinal tract is being healed
as we speak, loosened and cleared
in Jesus' name. My hands grow
moist in the prayer circle. *In Jesus' name,*
Mom whispers, as Pat tells us
there are many suffering from demonic depression,
feeling hopeless and scared. *We banish the suicidal spirits*
in Jesus' name, we banish them from your lives.
My knees burn against the thick carpet,
which looks like spilled noodles. *In Jesus' name,*
Mom whispers, as Pat tell us
we will find joy in the Holy Ghost. There is an impacted tooth
—not a wisdom tooth, but it's causing
great discomfort: *And Christ*
is healing you now; you feel the heat
of healing in that tooth. And I swear

I feel it up my legs and, *There are blisters*
on a forearm, Pat says. *You don't know where*
they are from, but they are vanishing
as we speak. With this, I look up from my prayers,
wondering if it could mean Grandma. But
if Mom thinks Pat's prayers
have reached the right ears
to save Gran, she gives no sign,
looking as she always does
when communing with Christ, as if having
the most pleasant dream. Pat Robertson
ends the prayer circle with an *Amen,* draws
away from the million living rooms, the thousands
of broken backyard windows and carpets soiled by cats.
He'll spend the next hour telling us
about the fetus farms that are planned for Missouri
and the computer chips the New World Order
wants to plant in our wrists. Only Christ
can save us from our doomed flesh, only our donations
can deliver us from this cursed earth.

Origin

For HTS

You give Jack your extra PB & J sandwich
because he left his lunch in his dad's car.
On the second bite, he gags, reaches into his mouth,
pulls a staple that was meant for you from the back

of his throat. A long metal quill between
his thumb and forefinger, a bead of red ink.
He places the bloody staple on a napkin
and you both get on with lunch. This is normal:
two losers—one bleeding from the mouth—arguing
about the best choose-your-own adventure stories. Horror
is the little things: a dot of blood
on a lunch napkin, the small hatreds
of your classmates. The reasons:
Your haircut. The shoes you buy.
The way you smell.
You will work at it, though.

When you are sixteen, you'll drive them
home. You'll bear the forty-five minutes
of ridicule until one passenger
is left and then, that particular silence
of being alone in a closed space
with someone who really
doesn't like you—a wasp nest

just outside your bedroom window. You'll chat
about The Doors and Floyd; and when
he says *later,* you'll feel good. Tomorrow
is a new day. Unwritten. And in gym class
when he tries to jab you in the ribs
with a forty-pound weight bar while others
hold you down, you'll tell yourself that
this is his way of letting you know
you belong.

Satanic Panic

In 1985, *60 Minutes* host Ed Bradley
sits down with Dungeons & Dragons co-creator
Gary Gygax, asks him,
If you found twelve kids
in murder suicides
with one connecting factor,
wouldn't you question it? This is the 80s, after all.
Ozzy Osbourne is sending
suicidal messages to teen boys and ten-year-olds
are shouting at their mothers
from the rumble seats of Custom Cruisers:
He-Man is the master of the universe now, Mom,
not God! Beelzebub is waiting in the Ouija boards
to possess teen girls just to spite Oral Roberts,
who has to put on his Saturday night slippers
and shuffle to the front porch
where stricken youths have gathered
and say: *I cast ye out in the name*
of Jesus! Psalms 8:2,
from the mouths of babes
come stories of tunnels under
daycare centres, of cellar stairs leading
to shrines covered in chicken blood.
And Halloween is pagan! The moon
is red! The Second Coming
is going to be wonderful,
and your second cousin
down in Buffalo

has got demons in him again
from all those damn games
and heavy metal garbage.
And Gary Gygax looks at
Ed Bradley, hunches
his shoulders, his voice
already way down the hall. He says,

Of course, I'd question it,
but none of this is scientific;
this is not scientific at all.

Be It as It May

When I was eight, I dreamed my family had died
and were floating away on a cloud terrace. They were noble
in bliss, hands waving as if from a parade float, unaware
of my cascading terror as I stumbled after them,
burdened by my living skin. The dream
left an impression, a bruise of thought: If death
could consume a whole family without fuss,
then what about one boy? How easy could it be
to just die, accidentally rip through the chrysalis
like a screen door in July? For months after, I had trouble
sleeping. I dreaded putting on, or taking off, a tee-shirt
because it meant having to close my eyes—and what
would happen if I opened them in the afterlife?
I did not want to go to Heaven or become a blissful butterfly
—a pair of wings with painted eyes meant to fool
larger prey. Here was fine. Eventually I slept, but the notion
of death being a matter of stumbling
on the front steps or swallowing a fishbone
caught me in its slow ferocity, its jaw-
spanning years. And now I wake up too early

in a low-watt fright. I'm not supposed to be here
to witness this: My life being consumed
without much fuss.

Blessed Defeat

I was ten, black-eyed and nauseous
in the back seat of an Oldsmobile
that smelled of wet dog and spilled
Double-Doubles on the way home
from the optometrist.
He told us—after I vomited
into a plastic receptacle
that looked as though
it had been intelligently designed
for nauseated optometry patients
—that the tennis ball
had caused no permanent
damage and the nausea
was due to the pain, and this
is when my mother
must have concluded
that the time was right—here,
driving home, up Yonge Street—
that I let Jesus into my life. A hostile
schoolyard game of Red Ass
had led me to this moment; and gladly
I accepted, asking
the Son of Man
to be my Saviour and,
if he had the chance, to loosen
the blessed vice-script
around my eyeball a little?
But this is not to say

I would have resisted
otherwise. I was a momma's boy and believed
everything she told me: about her haunted house
back in England, our demon-possessed
cousins in Buffalo,
a powerful computer at NASA
that disproved a cosmos
without God. *Not in 37 universes,*
it had said.

          I had clearly demonstrated my faith
in her world; but not until
I was in such a state that anywhere
but in my body was preferable,
was I really ready. No one comes to Jesus
whole.

No Easy Way

All the boys show up for the first day of Grade 7
with bleach in their hair and safety-pins
in their pant-cuffs; I am wearing yesterday's
socks and underwear, and this
is where the truth begins—a thread
like a scalpel. From Filene's Basement
to the Warwick Antique Market, the road
is cut by the summer
leading into Grade 8. My toes
squirm in my new British Knights;
I had begged and Mom had thought
I would fit in more at school, and for a week
the runners soothed the feeling of waking
to find my belly jig-sawed with stitches.
Picasso unfolds the human frame, his surgeon's
stroke; my mother soothes her own fears
with prayer chains and second-hand china.
I will be forty by the time I've understood
that someone who always forgets
to do up their zipper will never make
a Cubist's approximation of cool. It took a city
of neon crosses and gold buddhas
to help me believe that
good things can happen. But still
there's the nylon fishing line attached to me,
attached to that kid who showed up uninvited
to a Grade 9 party—holes purposefully cut

into his jeans, the ends flapping open
like a surgery gone very,
very wrong.

Supply Teacher's Lament

For Mrs J_____ (and Henry Moore)

In art class
I hold the plug of the TV in the socket
so that the kids
can watch a video. I am wedged,
like a forgotten Klimt, between the stand-on-wheels
and the wall. Every time I let go,
the TV switches off. I don't know
how to fix this: I'm not really
their teacher, but a supply who doesn't
yet know—as I half-stoop
like a tall woman
walking a 3-year-old—that nothing
is really wrong with the cord or socket.
I want to watch Henry Moore's progression
from the conventional to the abstract, but instead
must settle for flute music and the voice
of the male narrator sounding
remarkably like that Canadian TV news anchor
from the 70s.

Later, on my futon at home,
I am half-way to becoming the Female Figure
Reclined. The artist hands
of my red wine are both reducing
and making me whole, a direct carve

in reverse—and oh my god
those fucking kids
had the remote.

        Thirteen years old and they refuse
to show disappointment that I cancelled
the field trip. I ask if they know why,
and from behind the phalanx of young faces—
all at once rigid and bored—a single arm,
both separating and joining
a body, rises lazily. *Mrs J_____,
is this about the TV not working?* I don't recall
how I respond, but I do know
that I try, fatally, for sympathy;
and with that, my transformation
is complete. In their eyes
I am no longer the supply teacher,
but an abstract female
        intercut with voids.

People Change but Only If You Give Them Room to Do It

quote on a changeroom wall

My old school's website sparkles
like an ad for Gap clothing.
I have never seen such happy
incisors. Every "throwback" photo
comes with the heft
of the changeroom door. The odours
of crotch
and bleach, the mosquito
whine of terror
when action
and consequence are suddenly
separated by whispers. A shout
when a fist
slaps the back of a shoulder. The lips
of the bigger boy curl. In this space,
he likes how impunity
fits him. His smile widens, tells you
how the next ten minutes
are going to go.

Outside my grown-up office
there is always a gym teacher
pretending not to hear.

Touched

My mother
received the Holy Spirit
in a tiny uptown office
crowded with worshippers
and grey folding chairs and
men who looked
like retired beat cops
ready to catch
her as she tipped back, as if
having stood too close
to the Eastbound train roaring in. Oh,
such power, an enormity
to be kept
in a purse when you're certain
that all the empty
parking spots are just
for you.
                          Years later, in the Vineyard,
they work on me
in teams—meaty hands
on my shoulders and neck,
lips at my ears—
thanking and praising as I too
thank and praise
and beg for lightning. *Oh,*

you received it, Mom says
in the car, hours later. *I saw you.*
You received it alright.

　　　　I say nothing. I look up
at the night sky, its innumerable
suns. Tonight, I will go home
terrified of the Devil,
with his Nasferatu hands
reaching from under
my bed.

Windstorm

In the panic grass, we hold hands and pray.
Grandma is in the hospital again and Mom shouts
Jesus' name from the edge of the old foundation wall.
Dad says we could lose the goddam farm this time.
I cast you out, Mom yells into the tumult;
and in chorus we lean in and repeat after her
—the oldest hollers and whoops for the Son of God—
as the long and green blades are blown flat around us.
In Jesus' name, Mom says, *I invoke a circle of protection
around this farm and this family*.
                                        Weeks later,
Grandma is home. The farm is still ours and we are radiant
over our fried egg sandwiches, recollecting how the wind
died suddenly and how we could feel Satan vacate.
                                        Dad is out
at The Baker's Dozen across from the Farmer's Depot.
He's buying more bags of day-olds to stave off
the money collectors.

For NM

You were the prettiest girl in grade nine,
and you asked if I was a virgin in front of everyone
at a school party. Every nail
twisting in the frame of that room
stopped and understood
its place. Maybe I stared too much in geography
and this—your question—was the knife
to every rough trespass twisting
in your young woman's memory; my boy's obliviousness
that evening, drunk as I was
off the whiskey I stole and sipped
from a dirty mason jar, represented how great
it must be
to never have to worry about such things. And
there I was with my bowl cut, silly zippo lighter,
and the rips in my jeans that I obviously put there myself.
You couldn't contain it, and it hurt me enough
that twenty-five years later
I looked you up on Facebook
in the hopes of seeing that you're no longer pretty.
You're still lovely;
your last selfie posted
three years earlier, in an oncology ward—
a fifteen-year-old's face
infused with the hard-earned joy
of a woman who, for a moment, forgets the world
and rings that bloody bell.

The nurses behind you
aren't looking up, but you're laughing
open-mouthed and—
for a moment (forever)—
you are oblivious to so
many things. Even the petty
and wounded boys
that still occasionally
haunt you.

Covenant

I think I've told you about this dream.
You were all babies and we were alone
in the house and a bad man came in, dressed
all in black. Oh, his face! It was absolute evil.
I scooped you all up and ran outside onto
the driveway. I'd never felt so helpless.

But then, another man came. He had jeans on
and a tee-shirt. And he was completely barefoot
just like your Uncle Sammy. He told me
not to be scared and he walked into the house.
There was a terrible noise. The ground shook and
everything went quiet. Then the good man—

it must have been Michael the Archangel
now that I think about it—came out and said
that everything was alright. Oh,
there was such a sense of relief. God was trying
to remind me, I think, that if I have faith,
he'll protect all of us.

Mom, when you were a child, men looked
down from the night sky and dropped fire
on the rooftops of your neighbourhood.
In the bomb shelter, you held on tight
to Nanny, who kept her broken arm a secret.
I imagine you, during the worst of it, asking

quietly for Jesus and Mary to help you.
I don't know if the Mother and Son of Man
saved you that night; but in your dreams, as an adult,
they send the protector of Israel to cleanse your
imagined home—as large a gesture as the parking spot
closest to the Royal Bank. I'm being snide, yes;

but then again, I have never been the object
of such human hatred—eyes, lidless and swarming
the stratosphere, twitching like moths against their
bell-shaped lenses, trying to burn me out of a hole
in the earth. If this were so, perhaps I too would find
a hymnal in every voice, and in every iris

a little staircase inviting me up.

Weekend Warrior

On a kids' placemat, Garfield the Cat runs
across a patch of sand in flipflops with a beach-chair
over one shoulder, a parasol over the other, and a string
of sausages trailing behind. The banner above him
announces the words WEEKEND WARRIOR. I'm ten,
with my mom, and I want the placemat. My father
is in his fifties and doesn't appreciate leisure.
He leaves the house on Christmas mornings
to deliver fruit baskets to city councillors. He hurries
into the TV room and stands stock still, fingers
twitching as *Saturday Supercade* blares away on CBS,
his eyes darting this way and that for something,
anything. This time it's a tangled extension cord.
He throws it onto my lap and tells me to wrap it neatly;
then immediately grabs it back, muttering how *no one
takes the time to do things properly.* Knuckles working
the impossible knots, he faces the window
with an expression of incensed bewilderment
—an aggravated ennui-by-proxy. He's worked so hard.
I don't remember whether my mother bought me
the placemat or not, but I expect she would have done so
with a resigned disquiet. The moon runs red
and false prophets abound. Do we need another toy?
Why tempt one more tribulation? We could all
be taken up today. My father at the window again,
working the knot of his tie, the pre-dawn when he escapes
his promise of a week at Virginia Beach to pray
with Pat Robertson. On the morning of the flight,

he dresses hurriedly in the dark. I wake to my mom
sitting up in bed with my sisters around her. Why
would he do this and shun an eternity in paradise?
Outside, I follow his footprints through the snow
—from the steps, past his Lincoln Continental,
to the bus stop. Public transit: an extra Hail Mary
to atone for his sins.

Huddle Up

The replacement started crying
a few sentences into his pep-talk. Life
before Jesus was undoubtedly unbearable. So, we got
our old youth pastor back. Which was cool.
He was, in my 13-year-old eyes, the older dude
down the hall in a Leafs jersey
who'd help out with the garbage when your dad
wasn't around. *Everyone worries*, he says, *about going to Hell,*
and he draws a circle on the whiteboard. *But what they don't*
understand—he draws flames around the circle—*is that*
we are already in *hell, and it's our job*
to get out. At school, someone
had just tossed my clothes onto the locker room floor
and told me that I stunk like shit. At the prayer

retreats, there were girls. I would try
to get a seat at their table
in the mornings and before prayers
and later, after the horseback rides,
when we would huddle on our knees, arms upon
each other's shoulders in the prefab temple
—whose fake grass carpet smelled of wet earth—
and call out to be touched
by the Holy Spirit. I was, and will always be
unaware of any scripture that involves receiving
the Holy Ghost while pitching
a pup tent. I'm sorry, it's just—I suspected
I would never be picked for the team.

The first day, my father had reached over and pulled
the back door of the station wagon closed
as soon as my feet touched the unbearable
pavement and Mom's saucer-sized glasses
shone red with sun as the Oldsmobile peeled away.

I am standing on the temple drive.
Hi, says a boy my age, taking my hand, *welcome
to the group.* He has the first set of teenaged eyes
I've seen in a while containing no hint of
malice or motive. *Oh*, I think.
This might be alright.

For CB

From one loser to another,
I really want to say that
I liked you. But this isn't a screenplay
about high school outcasts buddying up
to win The Battle of the Bands. They shoved me
into lockers and smacked the back of your head
in the halls; and I found you repellent
as the bullies did, the way a bystander
might hate the victim. We can't escape

the pecking order, I tell my adult self. I sit next to a man
at the Coxwell Branch Library
who can't stop snickering. His happy obliviousness
worries me.
                    You would walk into science class
giggling and announce, *I'm back and I'm bad!*
And you must have known
what would happen. I needed you
far from me. Your unalloyed giddiness
was infectious. One can only be so free.
I did not want to get kicked out of
another one of Meagan's house parties.

Jesus Loves Me

I love Him more than you or your sisters, Mom whispers
in the middle row of the temple. *And you will love Him*

more than me. She tells me that when I die
I will stand before the throne and God will demand to know

why I should be allowed into heaven. If, in my life,
I have shouted Christ's name from enough mountaintops,

the Son of God will appear at my side and tell the Father
that I have borne witness to his works. And when the time

comes before the Seals are broken and I am raptured up
to the city of pure gold, it will be because of

those mundane summer evenings when I was nine or ten,
when I'd lean out my bedroom window and shout,

Jesus Christ is my Saviour, into the twilight. Oh,
my mother's heart! Each time. *That he can have such faith!*

But really, I thought I was headed for a lake of fire
and Jesus would get me off on a technicality. He would have to,

as part of the deal. Jesus would owe me this. I humiliate myself
a few minutes each day, and he puts in a good word. Do what you

need to do, just don't let me burn. The kingdom of heaven
revealed itself to Mom when she was driving

through a rainstorm. *The clouds drew apart,* she said,
like our living room curtains, and there it was. I do not believe

Mom would have liked to know that my theatrics
were part of a plea deal; but really, I was terrified

and she was born into a world where Hitler
made the cover of *Time* and Churchill let India starve

out of spite. I grew up grasping
for lifeboats. So, it appears, is everyone else in this temple:

the youth leader who bursts into tears before getting
two words out; the new converts, always down in front and

waiting to be saved, held in their seats by sweaty ushers
with arms like pressed hams; my mom, with her English hands

demurely at her sides as she quietly presses inwards
for that soft cut in the curtain. And finally, the tall,

thin pastor reaching above everyone else, calling for God;
red-faced, as the tongues of flame reach higher.

The Seventh Sign

1988, Carl Schultz

I can't watch this, sorry, no, and I reach for the eject button.
This is, this is, I just can't. And Allan reaches for my hand,
C'mon seriously it's just a fucking movie, man. But
this is, this is glamourizing the return of Jesus, I want to say,
but Mom's words can't find my mouth, and all

that comes out is, *Bad, this is bad.* I am fourteen
and have just ejected Demi Moore from the VHS machine
and Allan looks at me like, *You're such a fucking loser, man,*
but he'll keep hanging out as long as his parents are fighting
and my folks leave their cash out in the open. My mom

—who has knelt in the dens of musty farmhouses
with housewives dressed like widows—says being born again
means being attacked. *Satan will come for you even harder
now, tempt you through TV and books, and take your friends
away because you have given your soul to God*

—*and Satan wants it.* And I grip the video cassette
to my chest and shuffle-run out of the room. Allan snorts,
heads to the kitchen to make another sandwich
and rummage around for whatever
loose change he can find.

I'm Right Here

She is pale and thin and wears unironically large glasses
and thick leggings under her school kilt. Her frizzy hair
is always tied in a thick braid no less frizzy, and from where
I am sitting, she just tripped over her feet trying to get
the basketball from you in an intramural match.
You are a very popular guy—upper middle management
at least—and you've just planted your foot right
next to her head and you look down at her and, hold on,
did I mention that her last name sounds a lot like "donkey"?
And you crack the smallest smile and replant your right foot
on top of her thick ponytail momentarily pinning her
to the floor. You look around wondering if your friends
can see what you've done—pinned Donkey's head
to the floor with your foot! You don't look at me though,
never; you're always breezing right over my unkempt hairline,
and oh, how I need you to see that I am laughing.
That I am one of you guys.

The Temple

A young man stands
on the elevated platform
in the basement of the temple.
He wants to tell us a story—but first,
he turns his chair around
and sits on it backwards. He thinks
this story will save us.

We don't know this guy.
Our own parish sent us over
to listen. What we quickly learn,
was that he, at one time,
was a lady's man. He tells us

of his last dalliance, a blonde;
And fellas, she was fine,
he says to the teen girls
and boys in the room, his thumb
and forefinger crooked
into an A-OK. But when
she leaned in for a kiss,
he just couldn't.

And then he met The One.
She smiled, was always polite,
and at the end of their dates,
she would take a step
away from him
and say, "thank you."

At this point, another
young Christian male
ascends the elevated platform
and for the sake of clarity
demonstrates the Christian Side-Step,
which looks a lot like Charlie Chaplin
first setting off for a long walk
across the dusty roads
of Depression-Era America.

He remains onstage, and whenever
the former lothario says the word "guys,"
his new silent partner puffs out
his chest and draws an inverted
triangle into the air with his hands.
And when the youth pastor says the word "lady,"
the co-star performs a Betty Boop
and caresses an hourglass
from the air molecules before him.

This goes on for another thirty
minutes: the extolling of chastity,
the biting of imaginary bedposts
in bridled lust, the kissing of invisible pillows
in unvented passion.
The message is clear: We know
what it's like. And yet, if you wait, it will be totally

worth it. We didn't. Not us elders.
We dipped our toes in that exquisite tributary.
We filled our cups. But you—

your souls are not yours;
your bodies are temples,
paid for and pristine.
There is nothing more exquisite
than having not one sip, not one
taste before we let you.

Google

"Andrew Smith" and
"Holy Trinity School" and
"Richmond Hill, Ontario"
every few months when I am alone.
"Andrew Smith" and "England" and "drummer"
and "musician" on Yahoo when I was living
with Val behind the lady's salon
(our first day in the place, he says, *You know*
what that smell is? Burning hair!) "Andrew Smith"
plus "drums" plus "mountain bikes" plus
"classic Adidas high-tops" on Ask Jeeves
in a smoky PC room in predawn Seoul; I am perspiring
soju and nicotine and sentimentality. "Andrew Smith"
and "Licenced to Ill" and "The Number of the Beast"
and "rock band" and "England" on stationery
because everyone has a 386 now. *Dear Andrew,*
you need to accept Jesus Christ
as your Saviour because the moon
is running red with blood
and the end times are near, and I'll
never really get a reply to this letter.
Andrew Smith, you sprinted away
down the school hallway
—legs too long
for your pants—outraged
for the way things weren't, looking
for whoever gave Muhammad

a bloody nose. Andrew Smith, I've tried,
when the kids are asleep; but I have never
managed to catch up
to you.

What Balls

What do priests and Christmas trees have in common?
I ask the cabin of older Christian men. I am met with silence.
It had been an evening of good clean jokes. Now, outside,
leaves crunch under ghost weight and the spring
branches scrape against the outer edges of the shack.
Each in their bunk, the cocooned men wait.
And I—fifteen and friendless—also wait
till prompted by a *well, what?*

Their balls, I say, *are for decorational purposes only.*

There are a few things I remember:
the immediate guffaws and hoots of male laughter,
an arm like a large truckle of white cheese emerging
from a sleeping bag and repeatedly slapping the side of the bunk
next to mine, the thought that these people might like me.
And the gossip the following morning
—whispered across the breakfast table
by a girl with matching crucifix earrings—that
the owner, a god-fearing man built like a
pot stove, dresses up as a ninja at night
and creeps among the dry leaves and spring
branches, hunting for smokers, fornicators
and tellers of crude jokes.

So It Goes Further Into The Deepest Darkness

—Franz Kafka

You are dumb and brainwashed; I am lazy
and brainwashed (to be fair the lazy part
is very true). But you are also a rube and, yes,
I am a socialist whore and you tell me
to go to Russia if I like Big Government
so much, and I tell you to spend some time
in Somalia if you think we'd be better off
without it. This is Thanksgiving minus
the Thanks and the giving, the gun-loving
grandfather and the socialist
sockless uncle. We've never met,
but we draw our best guesses and then
beat the effigies with tube socks
full-to-bursting with facts. I demand
your sources, which I immediately dismiss
as invalid; you demand to know
how someone working in poetry
could possibly know anything
about anything. The amount of "mic drops"
and "checkmates" here could fill the canyon
between us, but then, why ruin the acoustics
with civility? Not sure about you
but I did not come here to change hearts,

I came to take selfies
in opinion form. The deeper
the gulf, the purer my voice is
to any follower who might
doubt me.

They Will Know Us

Every day, we are a little less supreme. Lisa says,
That's a lie, nobody really knows
the numbers. So, I meditate; try to formulate
another poem about Indonesia, about
those two dogs mating in the middle of
a busy road in Bali. I've never risked
a piece about two dogs fucking before, but
I've always envied their obliviousness
to everything except that act, the bumper
of a gentle car nudging them
out of the way. *We need more of us*
on the walls, you say. Just before
the coffee pot brews, another tantrum
by our youngest; another call
from a creditor. We've been quartered,
atomised by trivialities, and I want nothing. But, yes—
maybe to be deified next to a bay window, reborn
at the top of the stairs, whole amongst catamarans
and rice paddies and sunburned calves and cheeks.

Please Don't

Notes to Ava

In the playground, you show me a broken
bracelet you found and say, *Maybe those girls over there*
want to see it? I hold the pieces
and weigh their plainness against
this keen new want; you watch the older kids
as one would bite into a nearly ripened apple. I place
the bracelet between us on the bench and say nothing
to discourage you. You're three and a half; you need to belong
and I must remember that I was much older
the first time I was shoved into a locker door and
called 'loser'. I should forget this; but when you take
a step closer, I touch your shoulder, suggest we play
hide-and-seek together. I count to ten slowly
to give you all the time you need
to make yourself invisible.

Losing Yahweh in Gananoque

Chet Raymo said that after death
there was probably nothing,
and I shut off Radio Canada.
Before that, it had been a pleasant
afternoon in Thousand Islands.
Well-fed Americans were unloading
from buses. Buffet lunches
were waiting on flat-bottomed
tour boats, the bows sinking lower and lower
in the sun. Through their stained glass,
the island churches looked empty
and full of day. *I'm signing up*

to go to Mars, I had told my ex
the previous morning, and she absorbed
the declaration like a night nurse interrupted
during a smoke break. This
was no longer hers to carry.
I drove two hours to Kingston
and skulked down Princess Street.
How could everything
carry on without me? I thought
to the 80-million-year-old mosquito bits
embedded in the vitrified sands
of my windshield. I hurried
from the waters
of Gananoque; and from Chet—his idea

already cleaving its way
drop by drop
into my brain.

Move On

A 44-year-old man
should not entertain revenge fantasies.
He should not daydream
in public spaces about running into
a childhood bully in a crowded restaurant.
Introducing himself, waiting for the healthy flesh
around the old classmate's eyes to loosen
in recognition—this is so childish—
then slowly, calmly spitting into
the man's mussel linguini. His wife and kids
would be there too—please stop—watching
like eighteenth century portraits
with the eyes cut out. Daddy,
who is this bad man? Rocco,
what the hell do you think you're doing? No,

there must be distance between the poet
and the speaker. This
cannot get personal. The way

you treated me, N_____.

Death by Prayer Wheel

There is no 'why', the saying goes,
coined by the Nazi who took the icicle
from a Jewish prisoner and broke it
in half. Hear that, and you say to yourself:
I understand the gun then, truly.
Give me a little warmth, it says,
and I will be the terminal point,
the full stop to the lies they tell,
the fifty-seven ways they steal.
I am impunity's fountain pen
and your fingers on me are prayer notes
wedged into books fat with scripture. Touch,
spin the chamber so that the world can hear
your prayer: *Give me what I'm owed.*

Billions and Billions

—*Carl Sagan*

She tells me vampires and ghosts *aren't real life*.
When I ask her why she wants to watch me play
a zombie video game, why she isn't scared, she says,
Zombies are only in movies. She doesn't know about the idea
of a soul (or the horned monster that wants to take it
to his house of fire under the ground), but thanks
to a free Baptist day camp, she knows about Jesus
and now refers to the time before she was born as
when I was in the sky (which isn't entirely untrue).
She thought, for a while, that graveyard angels
were fairies, and is still wholly unaware of their demonic
counterparts, which lie in wait to possess her body
and take (again) her soul (again) to the house of fire
under the ground. She goes to sleep with a turtle-shell
nightlight casting stars on the ceiling, and occasionally
I remind her that many stars are suns that are very,
very far away; and she says nothing to that, already
drifting off, her body an ellipsis on a fresh page, each point,
each bit of her a mote of dust from a vanished star.
My daughter goes to sleep (unlike me)
with the door closed.

This Is What Life Looks Like
Some 200 Miles Above the Earth

After four hours of half-sleep, my ocean waves on loop
sound like dry leaves being sucked into a mulcher.
November 10, 2016: The moon, says the Space Channel,
is closer than any time in the last 68 years. Astronomers
couldn't care less, but white dudes are gleeful—spend hours
digitally enlarging it to triple its circumference,
then post it to Tumblr. I look at the man on the moon,
his big, round Cheeto face superimposed over
my diminished city and immediately I have rage fantasies
about crushing the testicles of skinheads on the subway.
But these men really won't be veiny dildos in jean shorts.
They will be schlubs with finger-stains
down the front of their shirts; out of their mouths will erupt
the invectives of well-fed old men on swivel chairs. Bald men
looking like Captain Underpants—if Captain Underpants
had anger management issues and showed up at Save America
basement meetings with stories of armed black youths
and towns in the Midwest gone to Sharia law because, hey,
dulce et decorum est. It is sweet to lie for a country you invent
while remembering it, and it is only proper to switch out
"Mexican" for "Muslim" when spreading the word
north out of Missouri: *pro patria mentiri.* Calm down,
they say. The swastikas on windshields and doors
are just pranks. Give it a chance, they say. The White Power
fliers in the park aren't really racist. And what? Did you
forget about Hillary's emails already? They ask,
still shaking with anger.

New World Order

dream senryus

The bus roars. Pagan girl
sits close; lips to my ear, oh—
sweet blasphemy.

Crash. The air hangs with embers;
autumn in Hell. My hands burn
off her dress.

In the Second Coming,
secret places to kiss
are the first to go.

Old barns fear our lust,
sheds would sooner collapse
beneath us; their nails shriek.

Now, the world chants in tongues.
Her gods are opened throats; mute
as cut flowers.

Relativity

Cheek by jowl on the morning train and reading Darwin
as he goes on about discoveries in local pigeons,
mollusks in the South China Sea, how the shape
of a beak reveals there's so much more to everything
than what Sunday morning in starched shirts
has been telling us, the billions of years it took
for the stones in our garden to get there
—minus the two hours Lisa and I had to drive
in order to steal them from the ruins
of the farmhouse, overgrown with weeds. You didn't exist

a second ago, Matilda, then here you are,
a copy of *Brown Bear, Brown Bear* above your head, yelling
Uk! Uk! and in every cell of you, the ashes of stars.

From Penuel to Jabbok (Wrestling the Angel)

1.

HULK HOGAN

The love that you give is equal to
the love that you receive
and that's the same with hatred
brother, you whisper-scream
from the wooden Magnavox
into our TV room, fingers splayed out
and reaching for a face. And for a second,
we are all heels getting a lesson in love,
Corinthians 13:13; and bouncing
from pec to oily pec,
the son of man dangles
from a gold chain—Christ
making his glorious return
on waves of Tampa Bay
muscle. Did I follow
the Three Demandments of Training,
Prayer and Vitamins? Would I be redeemed, walk in
the light of God's love? It's the eve of Wrestlemania 5,
and I don't know where Hulkamania ends
and the New Jerusalem begins.

2.

TERRY BOLLEA

Ultimate Warrior gorilla-presses you
above his head, strips you
of your belt. The pillars
in the heart of every Hulkamaniac
crumble. It will take years
before Delilah cuts your hair, the Philistines
blind you. A woman
named Clem. Her husband: Bubba the Love Sponge.
He records everything,
even the pillow talk when you use the N-word
repeatedly to describe your daughter's boyfriend.
The details of the sex tape
are released and you tweet
that, in the storm, God and his universe
will sail you where he wants. In the courtroom,
the same crucifix dangles between the lapels
of your expansive black suit—Jesus is still so far out.
For 30 years, replies @cdladiesnight,
I've been training, saying my prayers, and taking my vitamins.
You're not my brother anymore. How you've gone

from sun giant to furrowed village
priest. You have the shoulders
of one who's milled his own flour. Your eyes
have stopped seeing
that the parish dwindles. You no longer notice
how the graveyard grows
a little more each year.

I Had No Need of That Hypothesis

—P.S.L., 1884

What was said
between Napoleon and Laplace
is disputed. The exchange
was first recounted by Arago, who was in the room
at the time, to Hugo, who of course
spread the news. *So, where is God
in all this*, His Imperial Majesty allegedly demanded
of Laplace, who had just presented the Emperor
with news of celestial mechanics. How can this be (a version
of the encounter suggests)? *You made the system
of the world, you explain
the laws of all creation, but in all your book
you speak not once
of the existence of God!* Understand
that His handiwork is on every hair
of every head, on every grain of sand,
on every jot and tittle and lonesome
iota. Nothing lacks His fingerprint
and that which lacks
is nothing. *So, what am I looking at—*

this, my mother's expression
after reading my concrete poem
on language being a veneer
over a void. *Is this all you think*

of the world? She asks softly. She has
tried, really. And one day
one of your kids just ups and says there is nothing,
as if the Mona Lisa painted herself. How is it (an alternative
translation suggests) you say so much
about the Universe and nothing
about its creator? Can a tornado toss together
a functional jumbo jet
from scrap metal? The secular have

their hells. Multitudes, in fact. Tiny
and hypothetical, the result
of accidental collisions. All Laplace had wanted
was to talk about
the variations in the orbits of Saturn
and Jupiter; and what he got was
a room with an irritable Sun King,
a singularity holding infinite possibilities. Yet
out of the mathematician's mouth
comes a diamond. My mother
would not be bought
by such cleverness; and although
what I said has since vanished
into one of infinite hells, in all the realities
since I am visited by countless pastors, I am called
by an endless line of sisters,
worried for my souls.

A Sharp Stick

Dad never spoke about God, but when pressed
he would talk about his father
visiting him in a dream on the last morning
of a decade-long depression. *Get up, Vito,*
says the spirit; and Dad rises from the putrid bed,
takes the phone from Harriet's hand and tells Tony Salucci,
We don't owe you any money, in fact you owe me
fifteen thousand from the Brimley deal
goddammit. Slams the phone down, gets the keys
and drives to Lester Cook's house down the road.
And before Lester can say boo: *You saddamabitch,*
I took care of you for years, now I'm gonna tear
a stripe off you for what you did. Drives home, changes
out of his pajamas. Pulls out the phone book. *Phil!*
Long time no see. Whaddaya say we make some
money, huh? What do you learn

                              as a child, when your cousin
eats your favourite cat? When you hear men
being whipped in the town square? Your first good cry,
and God can't stand the racket; leaves you
with some dry hills and a dull knife, says, *Here,*
go make something of yourself.

Nothing Means Nothing, Yeah

For the Macho Man Randy Savage

I am talking all the way to the top!
You announce to Mean Gene
from behind your white-framed ski glasses,
which match the white-framed ski glasses
printed on your purple tee, the word
"Macho" in black below. *Unjustifiably*
in a position that I would rather not be in,
but the cream rises to the top! A wave
of your hand and a mini cream
container appears on your head,
topples off. You point your pinky
into God's ever-open eye. *On balance*
off balance, it doesn't matter, I'm better
than you are. A voice like a steel drum
being dragged across gravel. You were unworthy
of The Rapture, and deliberately so.
Even in your casket, your brother Lanny
would say you had that look. Feuding with heels
and babyfaces alike, you won your matches with rolls
of quarters, and lost with such open agony
that everyone loved you and was a little afraid
of the way you twitched like a power box
in a heat wave. Bruce Campbell
could find no escape from the noise
of you fucking your "acting coach" on the set

of Spiderman. Body-slamming a fan
for asking for an autograph, picking a fight
with a police dog in a Waffle House—the Four Horsemen
and Seven Seals be damned, the tribulations
would have been fun. So God, prima donna
that he is, reaches down and plucks
your swollen nihilist's heart as you drive
a Florida State Road. Your kingdom comes
as the SUV leaves the asphalt and slams you
gently into a palm tree.

Inconsolable

She follows me
screaming from room to room
because the floor is lava;
the chairs, cushions are full
of spiders; and my arms
are a green meadow
full of violets. When was
the last time I was that
scared? And when was
the last time I felt
this safe?

Batman V Superman

"When gods wish to punish us, they answer our prayers."
—Oscar Wilde

that little boy
looks at me as
he is dying
his final minutes
trickle along a fine
subaqueous thread
to a patch of pixels
on my monitor he is
expiring above a video
where two well-fed thirtysomethings
offer the third critique
of Batman V Superman
and below a pic of a grumpy cat
electrons are carrying the boy's
last breath over the mid-Atlantic abyss
even as he stares into the lens
gulping air scorched by rocket-fire
he is drowning in his poisoned lungs
and I won't unmute his passing
the rattle
in his chest that I imagine
is a divination
bones across wood
coward that I am

I can't
I won't listen as they knock
the gods
who allowed this
are finally answering
(whose prayers?)

A Father's Lament

I am the sleeve
of your parka, twisted
on the inside; the single
mitten; the pajama bottoms
on backwards. At night,
when you call out for the one
who is away, I stumble in—
an assemblage of everything
that is not the warm field
of moonlit clouds you expected.
I am salvation in the form
of a plastic kitchen chair. You reel back, *No,
not you, not you.* I hold you close
enough for you to hear
my heart, and your perfect
how-could-this-happen cry
works its delicate surgery. We
do this until your voice rasps
and you've exhausted yourself
pushing me away. I lay your replete
form back on the bed, skulk into
the toy-cluttered TV room, and stare;
quiet, as the rough and crooked
bits of me nourish
your flawless dreams.

The Great and Little Speck

We are awake in a calamity that arrives
in the form of dusk at noon—the sky
is a flowing yellow bedsheet
caught on the treetops. We are not allowed
to look up, but the old man down the block
is giving everyone an opportunity. He sits
under a red parasol with his telescope—
a metallic barrel filled
with vacuum, burning
with distance. I show the girls
how to wink
and we take turns peering
through the keyhole
into a closet
in Grandma's house where I struck
moonstones together—darkness
except for the crescent
of my thumbnail in the glow. Above us

an ambivalence so great, I mistake it
for intimacy. The girls, on the other hand,
have made no mistake: The cosmos
is boring. Through the hole
they see crumbs on a tabletop, a thumb-smear
of ketchup. Children know everything
they need. In the backyard,
their fingers reach down
like roots into the cool dark earth.

We Come And Go All the Time

Notes to Matilda

Margaret Laurence said the river moves
both ways, Matilda. But you're two and don't care what
a "Laurence" is, so you wander out from under the tree.
You have a climber's gait and, as you walk,
the flat green field rises against you; and I'm filled
with a coward's hope that you'll tumble back into me.
But you're defiant and you scale the meadow to see
what the blue sky allows you. Someone once lied and said
that subterranean city rivers are guided by the sun's pull;
and I believe it's the same force that pulls paper boats
across seven minutes of space, the same
that draws mothers to touch their bottom lips
at kitchen windows and watch quietly. I was
defiant then, too—a fixed point in rainboots
commanding the currents as they flowed in
and out of the tunnel only minutes ago. I am
a fixed point now, years later;
rooted in a field, watching the sun
carry something precious from me.
I have yet to learn what to do
with my hands.

I'll Tell You All the News

One of my students hands me
a copy of *The Essential Neruda*
and says, here, teacher,
things in the world
aren't so bad.
              For my latest, I've collected
tweets of Israeli teen girls wishing death
upon Arab children, nine pieces
of advice from a battered woman
on how to hide from an ex, and a small
anecdote from my father
about a neighbour's son
slowly dying from rabies
in his cellar in Mussolini's Italy. I don't think
she is suggesting that I write about
'happy things'; reflections on my mother adrift
in an ocean of morphine may have elicited
concern about my
well-being. So, I read her book. There's a poem
                 about a Vietnamese woman
—now dead—hiding herself, her child,
and her breasts in the mud;
and I'm reminded of Pablo's poem
"I'm Explaining a Few Things"
when the bandits come through the sky
to kill children, and the blood
of the children runs through the Madrilène streets
without fuss, as the poet screams, *Come and see,*

75

come and see! Pablo,
this isn't healthy. Should you dwell?
                 There is something to be said
about pressing down on a bruise, but
I don't think
we should confuse that
with burning away our malignities
with light. I don't want to focus
on our cruelty; but sometimes
it's either that, or we wait quietly
until the flowers
of our houses erupt into bonfires
set by fascists.

Let the Little Children Come to Me

Jesus said unto Sister Mary Immaculate*
of the Grey Nuns, "If Number 56
cannot hold down the porridge
and vomits onto the floor, go to him
then, and beat him upon the head
and neck until he eats
what he vomited; for is it not written
that God reigneth over the heathen
that God sitteth upon the throne of his
holiness?"
        "Beat the boy," Jesus said
unto Sister Mary Immaculate,
"until he eats every last drop,
for I am the bread of life."

* Note: Sister Mary Immaculate (or Anna Wesley) was a nun at St Anne's
Residential School in Fort Albany, Canada. The true events in the poem were
inspired by the testimony of former student Andrew Wesley (no relation).

A Million Dead End Streets

I steal a spice jar from Mom's cupboard, pour out
the oregano and fill it with Dad's whiskey, then cram
the jar into the front pocket of my jean jacket. I walk
the twenty-five minutes to the food court at the mall
just to be near other fifteen-year-olds who fall silent
when I walk by. The kids stare right through
my Doc Martins, my acid wash jeans. The Canada Club
brings a wet flush to my face. This will happen
in various forms for years. I will drive miles
to wrong addresses, wait for phone calls in empty
parking lots, and sneak through the kitchen windows
and back doors of parties to where more than a few
people have already threatened to beat me up
if I come around. Nowadays, I groan inwardly

when other parents approach me, smiling, to talk
about playdates and pizza Fridays. I hide in the hallway
when there is a knock at the door, pressing my Dad-bod
into a dark pocket. One evening at seventeen, I squeezed
through heating ducts to sneak into a dance. I screamed
all night above the music, hugged and wrestled
until I tore buttons. I did this for years: fail to say
what was needed. Until eventually I did.

Somewhere along the line it must have happened
because I find myself now half-dozing on the couch
with grey in my beard, watching my oldest draw up
invite lists for her birthday party, eleven months

in advance. I hug her constantly to crush whatever devils of self-hatred might take hold, I peek between the blinds at a loud and tangled mass of teens across the way. What are they doing. What are they saying.

Why Now

For Neils Bohr

My older sister sits close, asks,
Did something happen to you, you know
to turn you off
God? It has been fifteen years
under the peaceful indifference of the cosmos
and back then,
when my beliefs were an ill-fitted suit, I might
have responded
to the question
with a Hitchens quip on the modest arrogance
of faith. But now,
under throatless starlight,
I shrug. No.
No prayers unanswered. No
lost dog. No grievance, singular
as a sliver. The process was a stretch of road
and city workers chiselling back the asphalt, metre by metre.
They offered their bluster at first
and then the mundanity of the millionth shovel-load
of nothing. It's work, mind you,
and patience. There are those who scoff at apples
and talking snakes as they bicker about 9/11 jet fuel
and steel beams, mumble
about The Muslim Brotherhood
and the next secret meeting

of ZOG agents. So, no.
                                There's no point
to this anger. No chest-puffing
from the deck chair this time. I say a few
ambiguous words about the moon
and Earth's orbit and then
leave it alone.

Noam Chomsky Whispers in Your Ear

It's alright. I understand. Netflix is easy. Changing
the trajectory of the planet, not so much. There are risks
out there pricklier than a jar full of hornets. And soft
is the couch at the end of the day. You know
a little more about the death squads in Quito
or the meaning of militant Salafism. I get it. So what?
They'll build a telescope in the Atacama
to peer into star nurseries; mothers will kneel
in the shadow of its lens and dig for the bones
of their disappeared. Poetry exists
without your words. I've spent decades
speaking to empty rooms, and now there is no town hall
in the country that can house my numbers.
It's the accumulation
of the tiniest actions, fingers turning the earth's loam,
that upsets the machinery. The astronomers perched
before the leviathan will scratch their heads
as, hundreds of feet below, little hands stir
the dirt and shake the stars,
digging up the truth.

Beautiful Scoundrel

Lie to me, Peter Popoff. I'll donate my valuables
and you can pluck what you can pawn
and chuck the rest, that's fine. You can wear the earpiece
if you want, and from your wife's lips backstage
to your lips at my ear, you can say my name.
Pay the second mortgage. Take my head
with both your hands like a coconut
and shake the tumours loose. I've never
danced sober, but I will samba and jive
while you javelin my cane,
shot-put my walker,
and suplex my C-PAP machine
onto your empty stage. Sermons
are boring. You've long since leapt
from the turnbuckle to the throng—
elbows deep in scoliosis and gout,
arthritic kneecaps and orders
to evict. Swaggart. Bakker. Haggard. All gone. Yet you
—an exposed con, a mountebank unbowed
before scandal—carry on, dispensing glossolalia
from grandfather lips to thousands
at every whistlestop. Peter Popoff, I know you're full of it,
but you give the best hugs.

Come And See

John 1:39-41

Thank you. Now I know
that the apartment building across the street
will offer the best protection against
nuclear fallout as long as it has
a sub-basement. I post the article
with the comment that I would proudly
be the first in the neighbourhood
to turn to cannibalism. This,
as the Commander in Chief sends
an aircraft carrier named Carl Vinson
to the Sea of Japan (or the East Sea, depending
on one's historico-political bias), and then
promptly loses it as Dear Leader posts a video
of what San Francisco would look like
during a nuclear attack. I try not to give
that wistful Obi-Wan look as I say that it's been
a long, long time since I've heard anyone utter
the phrase "better dead than red"
(or "better red than dead," depending
on your historico-political bias)
with any real earnestness. I think it was my father
who said the former as he dropped us off at school
after the usual tirade against Japanese imports. The latter
was muttered, more or less, by a classmate (out from under
his burgeoning sweaty moustache) as we panted and heaved

through the endurance component
of the Canada Fitness Test. *I hope Russia*
fucking wins. But Russians loved their children too much,
while we believed too readily the stories of their kids
being forced at gunpoint to spit on the Bible—this
back when Pat Robertson had only
an afternoon slot on WUTV. My mother
touching the screen as she prayed, we imagined
every Russian holding a Jew hostage in the basement
of his Moscow home because, as far as we knew, Russians
were either godless in Moscow or Christian
in a gulag. Forty years later, I'm godless
in Toronto and a little jealous that the screens I touch
deliver no such clarity. I miss Yahweh and Lucifer;
they stuck to their scripts while these two
well-fed buffoons bang pots and throw pencils
and demonstrate that the universe really belongs to
George Lucas and Jerry Springer. We could
all be vaporized tomorrow or live to witness
another episode of *The Big Bang Theory*
—complete annihilation for free or glorified mediocrity
at nine million dollars an episode.
It's a worrisome thing, not waiting for Armageddon.

O My People! Their Oppressors Are Children and Women Rule Over Them

Isaiah 3:12

My eldest daughter refuses
to flush the toilet
shouts, *No,*
I want you to look at it,
before running off, giggling
as her little sister yells, *I want*
new milk, from the dining table
while I scramble around the kitchen
in a tee-shirt and boxers, trying
to customize their spaghetti dinners. These are
the end times! The signs are everywhere. How many Seals
have been broken in this house alone
as I peel candy wrappers and Play-Doh
off my back? How many horsemen
have knocked and turned their red faces
from the uncomfortable sight of me
in my underwear wrestling the dog
for the screen door? And I said,
Come and see, and they looked
at their watches, said, *Oh my*
look at the time we really
have to be going. And really,
in the news, the Earth is sliding
further on its axis, faster

than scientists can track; and I imagine
roomfuls of partially bald men
studying the numbers. Used to being
in control. They stare worriedly
out of adamant windows as the centre
of the universe slowly slips
from under them.

Things Are Not So Good Right Now

Matilda, I want to tell you:
I was probably very annoying
in school. I think people
were mean to me but I …
                    Matilda! You cry all the time! Like
all the time. I'm sorry,
you can cry as much as you want.
It's my fault,
not yours. At school
sometimes I would say bad things,
like really bad things. Right now
we've got a politician
rubbing shoulders with a neo-Nazi
at a pro-pipeline rally, and he goes up in the polls
because it's 2019 and we need to explain
why Nazis are bad. I remember
I'd insert the word 'bitch'
into my sentences loud enough
for Ms. Thompson to hear me. Crude. And now,
thankfully, the neo-Nazi is drowned out
by Indigenous protestors, shouting *Nazi scum;*
and Matilda, I want to believe
that I didn't yell out the word 'rape'
in class, but I probably did. I want to believe
that I didn't tell a joke about the Ku Klux Klan
in class, but I probably did. Matilda,
you never say 'please' or 'sorry',
and maybe you shouldn't to people like me.

The pro-pipeline protesters
shout *commie scum* back at the Indigenous
folk, because it's 2019
and Indigenous folk are
communists now. Really
what have you got
to cry about? My grandfather
would threaten to give me something
real to bawl my eyes out over
if I didn't button up,
act like a man. It's 2019
and when I see your tears, I get scared
they'll cleave me in half like so many monsters
are trying to, but can't.
I get scared because you are
already in my crevices, Tilda;
and when you cry, all I can see
is more ocean coming in.

Lisa, We Cling to Them, Don't We

The turtle glows on my chest: sun giant
in its belly and stars cut from its back. The girls
on either side of me and you in the emergency room.
The evening has forgotten its lines,
tugs at its earlobe the way I did
as a child, standing on the front lawn
at 2 AM watching the church burn, the embers
touching distance. We hold up
our hands, sing *twinkle, twinkle*
to the ceiling.
                    In this new universe,
the girls are euphoric. Their voices crackle
with tears. *Will Mommy
be home soon?*

Tammy Faye Bakker Sings to Me

Don't give up, you're on the brink of a miracle!
She holds up a free hand, just as she was held
by the Lord and painted: the china-blue shadows of her eyes,
the ivory on her cheeks. A miracle
singing for miracles. Mom says
we'll have to eat canned food
for the rest of the summer. In the fields,
she stops what she's doing and prays.
Dad hauls in boxes of kidney beans
shouting about the goddamn
interest rates, the dregs of a wine jug
on his breath. There is precious little
like the moments before your favourite
cartoon comes on. Tammy knows. It's the roll
of the first thunder. I pull at my sock ends
as she crescendos (far from her Minnesotan wheat).
Mom says, *Why don't I start drinking too?* Then grabs
at the wine jug. Dad pushes her away. They square off
in the kitchen. We are so close. The boys
next door have quit school
to help their own father and praise the Lord.
Force Five Grandizer, the protector
of my heavens, flashes across the TV screen.
This Saturday morning, Tammy doesn't fail me.

We Are This Now

I am one tube sock. You are a stained tee. Seven years ago,
we were the latest Scandinavian indie song crackling
from a speaker in a lime-green kitchenette. Our laundry reeked
but it was creative, a melange of synonyms
our children have since broken into blunt
objects. I look at your head and say, *what a cute*
baby doll; you look at my feet and say, *dishes*,
and then our youngest rocks her skull back
into your nose again
and our eldest digs her knee-bones
into my genitals. We limp in the sun
from street fair to street fair with a wagon
with a broken front wheel—wordless.
In our pockets, friends string together manuscripts
about their cats and how difficult it is
to take care of them.

Any Wickedness, but the Wickedness of a Woman

Eccles. 25:13

Tilda, I want you to know that I can't trust you
and I love it—the way you look me in the eye
and tell me you don't know why
there are chocolate wrappers
all over the table
and under your chair. Not a hint
of culpability; as if Joe Pesci were five years old,
gorgeous, and a girl. This is business, Dad. A matter
of ideals, the rugged individual in conflict
with a world full of meddlers
that would keep me
from the things I want. Of course
Mom said I could have this bag
of chips. Did Ava say I could play
with her Hatchimal collection? Sure. There is nothing
personal about this. These are the facts,
Dad; alternative maybe,
but we cannot get distracted.
The crisis remains: The divide between me
and what I want cannot stand.

A Silent And Loving Woman Is a Gift Of The Lord

Eccles. 26:14-15

I want you to know, Tilda,
that despite the fact
that I grimace and pinch
the bridge of my nose and utter
things under my breath
as you trail behind me;
you are right to complain
that you're tired of walking, even before
we've exited the garden gate. And that your socks
feel funny. And that you don't want
to blow your nose. That your sister
won't share. That your sister
won't play. That you don't want
to play. That you never
get a treat. That sharing
is caring, Ava! That you hate
your sweater and your snowsuit.
And you never get to watch
YouTube. That I am not
the boss. That no one
is the boss. Sometimes,

I succumb to the temptation
And tell you to quit whining. Oh,
let's be honest,
it's more than sometimes. It's hard,
really hard, not to; and I know
I should let just you swing away
at the way things aren't. On every
screen, a principal is sending another
girl home because of her shorts, a bro
is trying to explain primates
to Jane Goodall, and another council
of old men make decrees on women's
bodies. It's God's plan, they say.
                    Tilda, I have to learn
to keep quiet while you stretch
and flex your disgruntled yawp
against the unfair kitchen walls,
the oppressive snowbanks,
the unjust bedtimes
we've set. Tomorrow

so very much needs
your tiny belligerences.

Forbidden

The drapes in the windows of my next-door neighbour's
house were white once. In secret, I scrape their glass
with fishbones, but still I cannot see the thick, scentless
ferns I know are inside. They thrive on low-watt light
and dust. I am blind to the promised land
where ivory-covered almonds (I will never taste)
sit for centuries in green-tinted bowls. Through

the dryer vent comes the smell of Sole in olive oil: Heaven.
I had made it to the threshold, but I become thirsty
and beat a rock for water instead of whispering to it.
We all drank, but I alone was kept out. Now I hear them,
my chosen, as they bicker in paradise; their righteous curses,
their elbows scraping like giants against the alley wall
between our homes on mornings so early, I see only myself
staring back. My eyes are phantom limbs; my face is a visage

of drowned marble. Sometimes, I feel I am among them
—my chosen—and that I am speaking the old tongue,
but in fact I am just stumbling around the wrong house
for a light switch. We've spoken, yes. I was joyful
at the chance; the old one pointed to the branch
on my mulberry tree, which grazed the eaves of their
house. *Cut, please*, she said, before turning away.
My other neighbour—an "unclean"—continually invites
me over to look at his new light fixtures. I know what
the subfloor to his bedroom looks like. I want to smite

the golden calf on his coffee table, but the long
chocolate eyelashes on that animal disarm me;
I've always been weak, that's the trouble.
I wanted paradise, but wanted exotic sweets, too.
I wanted to hate as purely as my brothers—diamond,
a rare jewel in the brain—but lacked the faith and loved
too clumsily. I am spent, a broken matchstick.
There is little for me now but *Seinfeld* reruns and the
final rooftop where Yahweh's thick, rude fingers await me.

Our Time

I wrote my last poem for you
seven years ago. I'm sorry, I got caught up
with things. The jaundiced cup-sized baby
we nursed with thimbles of milk
is now a white-belt
in Karate. Our second daughter,
born in a bathtub
on Christmas Eve,
is entering French immersion
next year. Our time
has become more than cardigans
and hand-held mirrors,
and impossibly more than
half-jars of rare seeds—those
artefacts I assigned to you
and you to me are now components
of a greater adventure. You

are my fingerprints, and I,
the soles of your feet. You,
my eyesight; and I
am every morning that you get out of bed,
nonetheless. We are
each other's instruments. I'm sorry
it's taken so long, but it's
so easy to lose myself
in the world
we've been building.

Mon-Fri

After Robert Creeley

I have yet
a name for this
sadness. Step off
the 111 bus

onto the overflow
road. Of all things
in my little world.
The shadows

that glide across
the Atlantic, far
outside the
choices

I have made. Have made me
a fixed point, my face attached
to the phone. I don't care,
I say to no one. Every

8:00 AM. In a minute,
I'll forget more ocean
than these seagulls
will ever see. And

there is power
in this. Hunch
the morning
into a black box, walk

across the empty
lot into the near-vacant
school. Not sadness,
I say to no one.

Defiance.

Lyric for the Dead

On May 18th, Norman Bellamy of North Charleston died, and I love him. On May 18th, Masahiko Chida, born in Japan, resident of Lihue, began his sleep of the soul, and I love him. I also love Marguinha Da Costa of Chinchinim, wife of late Joaquim Mended, who ate at the hearth of Yomi; and I love the God who called to his celestial kingdom our beloved unforgettable Laura de las Mercedes Ortiz Riquelme of Chile. In the arms of Jesus is Jacques Hanna Assets of Tripoli, Lebanon, husband of Nicole Fadauva, and I love him. Freed from entangled roots is Grace Inabinette Walker, 72, of James Island; and I love her as much as I embrace the departure of our friend and uncle, Nelson Orlanda Benavente de Mayo, the apple of my eye. Into the Third Realm is Roney Richard Dennis of Western Australia, loving brother of Frank (extinguished), Pauline (released), Don, and Cheryl, and I love him and Frank and Pauline. And I love Kenneth McCrae Adams of New Zealand, and I love John (Terry) Terence of the same. On May 18th, Margarita Gomez Aravena of Chile fell asleep, with everyone inside my heart.

We Know This Much

We open on the boy in the back of the van, hiding
his dog under a horse blanket. Enter the father, face
in the backdoor window. *Goddammit Rocco,*
I told you Ringo's a big dog and he's got to stay,
protect the farm. But Dad, he's a city dog, a retriever!
We want the kid
to say something more. Kick!
Make a ruckus! But the boy just watches
as his dog is pulled from the van. Useless.
A necessity, the father says, shutting the door.
We hear his footsteps, the driver's door,
the engine; and then fade out
as the dog runs in the rear window
and the boy watches his pet lose pace
with the van, his arm over the backrest.
Get a shot of the dog's eyes—no,
cut to boy instead, struggling with his schoolbooks
on the verge of tears from what
his mother has told him. Mrs. Forester
touches his arm, *Don't worry, Rocco*
they'll find your dog. Now cut
to Ringo
dying in the field behind the barn.
No one will see this. The dog moans, understanding little
but the pain and maybe
that this tall grass is not
his living room carpet. He whimpers once more,
softly, and we imagine his dog thoughts

winking out, one by one. We open on the boy
months later, a Sunday barbeque. Our camera
at the waistlines
of a circle of men. Heavy laughter,
and the father
at the centre. Even now,
we wait for an acknowledgement of such
a mistake—retriever as guard dog—but it will never be
in the language of the father to admit;
it will never be in the eyes of the boy
to demand. There is only
their lasting mutual silence, two closed doors,
and something precious buried in a field.

On Your Third Straight Visit to the Walk-In Clinic

Daddy, what happens
after we die? A very rational response
percolates in my mind
about living on
in people's memories, but by then
we arrive. You get out,
dragging your booster seat behind you,
and I see the look on your face. Sweetie,
remember, you're not getting a needle today.
There's the sound of tires
over wet asphalt, like freighters
slipping upstream.

                     I'm not
worried about shots, you say, each word
a small ballast: I am afraid
of more bad news.

I am your dad. I am a ration-box
of facts, a survival guide
of practicalities
and small risks. But I know
you need Grandma now,
the quiet subaqueous ruins
she would bring to your
bedside. First there would be
the lap of waves
at your belly, and then you'd dive,
and down you'd go into tall tales

the temperature of blood.
Suspended in the warmth,
the ageless fables would
come into view; their enormity, their eyes adream
with Irish moss.

An Atheist's Lament

So, the earth is not a stepping stone.
There is no Club Med. No one
is saving us. Everything is a coincidence.
No one is born on purpose. Good people who die
in misery are never rewarded. The evil who die in comfort
are never punished. All it really takes is a couple of zealots
with box cutters, one slip in the shower, one gamma ray
burst in our direction. We are all on ice as thin
as our blood brain barriers; and beneath
is the lost moment we placed our keys down
somewhere, stretched on into forever. So, we cannot

waste time. No bowl of ice cream while staring
into space. No *Office* reruns. No Candy Crush.
No sharing Baby Yoda memes. No shaking dandruff
onto the desk. No Twitter feuds while lying in bed
at 9:20 AM. No YouTube videos of bass guitar covers
or corgi pups tumbling on a moving sidewalk. No
midnight Megabus to Atlantic City. No fourth helping
of battered shrimp at the Mandarin. We cannot 'just' grab
a coffee. Time grinds us to a fine, finite point;
and we are both the eyes in the sharp hours
and the precipice over which we stare
—precarious and drunk on the ambivalence,
the grandeur, and the choices
that don't even know
we exist.

Notes

"From Penuel to Jabbok (Wrestling the Angel)": Terry Bollea is Hulk Hogan's real name.

"Beautiful Scoundrel": Peter Popoff, as of 2017, is an active televangelist and faith healer.

"Lyric for the Dead" is comprised of information gleaned from obituaries from around the world for deaths on the single day of May 18th, 2017.

Acknowledgements

I would like to thank Guernica Editions for publishing my collection.

Thanks to my wife Lisa Keophila for your support, Anna van Valkenburg and Jacob Scheier for your editorial advice, and Rafael Chimicatti for the wonderful cover design.

Thanks to the Toronto Arts Council, the Ontario Arts Council and the Canada Arts Council for giving me the time and place to write.

Thanks to all the literary journals that have published poems from this collection:

Prairie Fire, "I'll Tell You All the News", published as "Let Me Tell You Something" (poem), Volume 43, No. 2, Summer 2022.
Ephimiliar, "Ever After" (poem), https://ephimiliar.com/magazine/, April 2021.
Prairie Fire, "Oh My People" (poem), Vol. 41, No. 3, Whole No. 172, October 2020.
Antigonish Review, "We Come and Go All the Time," (poem), Issue 196, 2018.
Canlit, "Mon-Fri" (poem), 234, Autumn 2018.
Grain, "So it goes further into the deepest darkness" (poem), Vol 44.4, Summer 2017.
Prairie Fire, "We Are This Now" (poem), Vol 38, No. 1, 2017.

About the Author

ROCCO DE GIACOMO has published several poetry collections, including most recently *Every Night of Our Lives* and *Brace Yourselves*. His poems have appeared in literary journals and anthologies in Canada, Australia, England, Hong Kong and the US. Rocco has been a member of the Coordinating Committee for the bpNichol Chapbook Award, a member of the Art Bar Poetry Series, and he has been commissioned to write poetry for the CBC. Rocco lives and writes in Toronto with his wife, Lisa Keophila, a fabric artist, and his daughters, Ava and Matilda. *Casting Out* is his fourth full-length collection.

Printed in January 2023
by Gauvin Press,
Gatineau, Québec